THE BATTLE OF AUGHRIM

and

The God Who Eats Corn

THE
BATTLE OF AUGHRIM
and
The God Who Eats Corn

by

RICHARD MURPHY

FABER AND FABER
24 Russell Square
London

First published in mcmlxviii
by Faber and Faber Limited
24 Russell Square London WC1
Printed in Great Britain by
The Bowering Press Plymouth
All rights reserved

SBN 571 08724 8

ACKNOWLEDGMENTS

THE BATTLE OF AUGHRIM was commissioned by the B.B.C. Third Programme, and first broadcast on Radio 3 in August 1968. The readers were Cyril Cusack, C. Day Lewis, Ted Hughes, Margaret Robertson and Niall Toibin. Music was composed by Sean O'Riada, and played by Ceoltoiri Chualann under the direction of the composer. Douglas Cleverdon produced the programme.

Parts of the poem have appeared in the *Listener*, the *New Statesman*, the *Irish Times*, *Hibernia* and the *Massachusetts Review*.

THE GOD WHO EATS CORN has been revised since it first appeared in the *Reporter*, the *Listener* and *Penguin Modern Poets 7*. A reading by the author was broadcast on the Third Programme in August 1964, produced by George MacBeth.

THE BATTLE
OF AUGHRIM

The battle of Aughrim (literally *horse-ridge*) was fought on the evening of Sunday 12th July 1691 about 17 miles south-west of Athlone, almost in the centre of Ireland. It was the last decisive battle in Irish history.

The Irish army was a native force, equipped by Louis XIV, and commanded by the French Marquis of St Ruth. Paid in brass, it fought in the name of King James II, an exile at St Germain, and in the Catholic interest.

The English army, aiding the planters in Ireland, was largely a force of foreigners, drawn from seven nations opposed to Louis, and commanded by a Dutch General, Baron Ginkel. Paid in silver and gold, it fought in the names of King William and Queen Mary (nephew and daughter of James), in the Protestant interest.

Since the previous summer, when James had been defeated by William at the Boyne, the Irish Jacobites continued to hold out in Connaught, led by the ageing Viceroy, the Duke of Tyrconnel. Patrick Sarsfield, Governor of the western province, a Major-General of the army, had saved the besieged town of Limerick by a daring raid on William's supplies in August. But though James had given Sarsfield the title Earl of Lucan, he had appointed a Frenchman Commander-in-Chief of the Irish army. St Ruth arrived at Limerick in May, lost Athlone by vanity and carelessness in June, and decided to stand at Aughrim on the 12th July to restore his position and redeem his name.

Patrick Sarsfield disputed this hazardous strategy: his policy was to avoid risking the remnant of his nation on one great combat. St Ruth dismissed Sarsfield to the rear of the army, to command the reserve, and gave him no information about the battle. The Irish, strongly placed on the hill, held off the allied onslaught until St Ruth's decapitation. Then a traitor, Colonel Henry Luttrell, withdrew his cavalry from a vital pass. Sarsfield could do no more than cover the retreat to Limerick, where he signed the Treaty, and in October sailed to France with 10,000 troops (known as the Wild Geese) to join the Irish Brigade. Two years later, a *maréchal-de-camp*, he was mortally wounded at Landen in the French victory over William of Orange.

I
NOW

Who owns the land where musket-balls are buried
In blackthorn roots on the eskar, the drained bogs
Where sheep browse, and credal war miscarried?
Names in the rival churches are written on plaques.

Behind the dog-rose ditch, defended with pikes,
A tractor sprays a rood of flowering potatoes:
Morning fog is lifting, and summer hikers
Bathe in a stream passed by cavalry traitors.

A Celtic cross by the road commemorates no battle
But someone killed in a car, Minister of Agriculture.
Dairy lorries on the fast trunk-route rattle:
A girl cycles along the lane to meet her lover.

Flies gyrate in their galaxy above my horse's head
As he ambles and shies close to the National School—
Bullets under glass, Patrick Sarsfield's *Would to God* . . .—
And jolts me bareback on the road for Battle Hill:

Where a farmer with a tinker woman hired to stoop
Is thinning turnips by hand, while giant earth-movers
Shovel and claw a highway over the rector's glebe:
Starlings worm the aftergrass, a barley crop silvers,

And a rook tied by the leg to scare flocks of birds
Croaks as I dismount at the death-cairn of St Ruth:
Le jour est à nous, mes enfants, his last words:
A cannonball beheaded him, and sowed a myth.

2

I dream of a headless man
Sitting on a charger, chiselled stone.

A woman is reading from an old lesson:
'. . . who died in the famine.

Royal bulls on my land,
I starved to feed the absentee with rent.

Aughrim's great disaster
Made him two hundred years my penal master.

Rapparees, whiteboys, volunteers, ribbonmen,
Where have they gone?

Coerced into exile, scattered
Leaving a burnt gable and a field of ragwort.'

July the Twelfth, she takes up tongs
To strike me for a crop of calf-bound wrongs.

12

Her weekly half-crowns have built
A grey cathedral on the old gaol wall.

She brings me from Knock shrine
John Kennedy's head on a china dish.

3

In bowler hats and Sunday suits,
Orange sashes, polished boots,
Atavistic trainbands come
To blow the fife and beat the drum.

Apprentices uplift their banner
True blue-dyed with 'No Surrender!'
Claiming Aughrim as if they'd won
Last year, not 1691.

On Belfast silk, Victoria gives
Bibles to kneeling Zulu chiefs.
Read the moral, note the date:
'The secret that made Britain great.'

Derry, oakwood of bright angels,
Londonderry, dingy walls
Chalked at night with 'Fuck the Queen!'
Bygone canon, bygone spleen.

After the noose, and the black diary deeds
Gossiped, his fame roots in prison lime:
The hanged bones burn, a revolution seeds.
Now Casement's skeleton is flying home.

A gun salutes, the troops slow-march, our new
Nation atones for her shawled motherland
Whose welcome gaoled him when a U-boat threw
This rebel quixote soaked on Banna Strand.

Soldiers in green guard the draped catafalque
With chalk remains of once ambiguous bone
Which fathered nothing till the traitor's dock
Hurt him to tower in legend like Wolfe Tone.

From gaol yard to the Liberator's tomb
Pillared in frost, they carry the freed ash,
Transmuted relic of a death-cell flame
Which purged for martyrdom the diarist's flesh.

On the small screen I watch the packed cortège
Pace from High Mass. Rebels in silk hats now
Exploit the grave with an old comrade's speech:
White hair tossed, a black cape flecked with snow.

I drive to a symposium
    On Ireland's Jacobite war,
Our new elite in a barrack-room
    Tasting vintage terror.

Once an imperial garrison
    Drank here to a king:
Today's toast is republican,
    We sing 'A Soldier's Song.'

One hands me a dinted musket-ball
    Heated by his palm.
'I found this bullet at Aughrim
    Lodged in a skull.'

Slate I picked from a nettlebed
Had history, my neighbour said.

To quarry it, men had to row
Five miles, twelve centuries ago.

An inch thick, it hung watertight
Over monks' litany by candlelight:

Till stormed by viking raids, it slipped.
Four hundred years overlapped.

Pirates found it and roofed a fort
A mile west, commanding the port.

Red-clawed choughs perched on it saw
Guards throw priests to the sea's jaw.

Repaired to succour James the Shit
The battle of Aughrim shattered it.

Through centuries of penal gale
Hedge-scholars huddled where it fell.

Pegged above a sea-wormed rafter
It rattled over landlord's laughter.

Windy decades pined across
Barrack roof, rebellion, moss.

This week I paved my garden path
With slate St Colman nailed on lath.

7

Left a Cromwellian demesne
My kinsman has bulldozed three bronze age raths.

I remember a child fell dead the moon
Her father cut hawthorn in those weird rings.

Will his wife's baby be stillborn?
He wants his park to graze one beast per rood.

16

No tree can survive his chainsaw:
Hewing is part of the land reclamation scheme.

He's auctioned grandfather's Gallipoli sword
And bought a milking machine.

Slate he stripped from a Church of Ireland steeple
Has broadened his pig-sty roof:

Better a goat's-hoof in the aisle
Than rosary beads or electric guitars.

Five hundred cars pass the stone lion gates
For a civil war veteran's funeral.

On a grave behind a petrol pump
The wind wraps a newspaper around an obelisk.

On ancient battleground neat painted signs
Announce 'Gouldings Grows'.

8

A side-car creaks on the gravel drive,
The quality arrive.

With Jordan water
They mean to give me a Christian start.

Harmonium pedals squeak and fart.
I'm three weeks old.

It's a garrison world:
The good are born into the Irish gentry.

What do they hope my use of life will be?
Duty.

Fight the good fight:
Though out of tune, if loud enough, it's right.

Under the Holy Table there's a horse's skull
Shot for a landlord's funeral:

From a religious duel
The horse cantered the wounded master home.

Two clergy christen me: I'm saved from Rome.
The deaf one has not heard my name,

He thinks I am a girl.
The other bellows: 'It's a boy, you fool!'

9

One morning of arrested growth
An army list roll-called the sound
Of perished names, but I found no breath
In dog-eared inventories of death.

18

Touch unearths military history.
Sifting clay on a mound, I find
Bones and bullets fingering my mind:
The past is happening today.

The battle cause, a hand grenade
Lobbed in a playground, the king's viciousness
With slaves succumbing to his rod and kiss,
Has a beginning in my blood.

II
BEFORE

I

BEFORE

The story I have to tell
Was told me by a teacher
Who read it in a poem
Written in a language that has died.
Two hundred and fifty years ago
The poet recalled
Meeting a soldier who had heard
From veterans of the war
The story I have to tell.

Deep red bogs divided
Aughrim, the horse's ridge
Of garland hedgerows and the summer dance,
Ireland's defence
From the colonist's advance:
Twenty thousand soldiers on each side,
Between them a morass
Of godly bigotry and pride of race,
With a causeway two abreast could cross.

In opposite camps our ancestors
Ten marriages ago,
Caught in a feud of absent kings
Who used war like a basset table
Gambling to settle verbal things,
Decide if bread be God
Or God a parable,
Lit matches, foddered horses, thirsted, marched,
Halted, and marched to battle.

'Gentlemen and Fellow Souldiers'
said the Marquis of St Ruth, addressing the Irish army with
a speech translated by his secretary, and quoted by the
Reverend George Story in *An Impartial History of the Wars
of Ireland*,

'I Suppose it is not unknown to you, and the whole
Christian World, what Glory I have acquired, and how
Successful and Fortunate I have been in Suppressing
Heresie in France, and propagating the Holy Catholick
Faith, and can without Vanity boast my Self the happy
Instrument of bringing over thousands of poor deluded
Souls from their Errours, who owe their Salvation to the
pious care of my thrice Illustrious Master, and my own
Industry, assisted by some holy Members of our unspotted
Church: while great numbers of those incourigable
Hereticks have perished both Soul and Body by their
obstinacy.

'It was for this reason that the most Puissant King my
Master, Compassionating the miseries of this Kingdom,
hath chosen me before so many worthy Generals to come
hither, not doubting but by my wonted Diligence I should
Establish the Church in this Nation, on such a foundation
as it should not be in the power of Hell or Hereticks here-
after to disturb it: And for the bringing about of this
Great and Glorious Work, next the Assistance of Heaven,
the unresistable Puisance of the King my Master, and my
own Conduct; the great dependance of all good Catholicks
is on your Courage.

'I must confess since my coming amongst you, things
have not answered my wishes, but they are still in a posture

to be retrieved, if you will not betray your Religion and Countrey, by an unseasonable Pusilanimity.

'I'm assured by my Spyes, that the Prince of Oranges Heretical Army, are resolved to give us Battle, and you see them even before you ready to perform it. It is now therefore, if ever that you must indeavour to recover your lost Honour, Priviledges and Fore-fathers Estates: You are not Mercinary Souldiers, you do not fight for your Pay, but for your Lives, your Wives, your Children, your Liberties, your Countrey, your Estates; and to restore the most Pious of Kings to his Throne: But above all for the propagation of the Holy Faith, and the subversion of Heresie. Stand to it therefore my Dears, and bear no longer the Reproaches of the Hereticks, who Brand you with Cowardise, and you may be assured that King James will Love and Reward you: Louis the Great will protect you; all good Catholicks will applaud you; I my self will Command you; the Church will pray for you, your Posterity will bless you; Saints and Angels will Caress you; God will make you all Saints, and his holy Mother will lay you in her Bosome.'

3

'Teigue in his green coat rides to war,
Nuts are swelling in the hazel-wood.
My father's ten black heifers low,
I've lost the father of my unborn child.

25

Last night he left me in a copse to weep
When foragers bugled there'd be a battle.
Proudly he gallops in Sarsfield's troop,
My tongue less to him than a drum's rattle.'

4

A country woman and a country man
Come to a well with pitchers,
The well that has given them water since they were children:
And there they meet soldiers.

Suspecting they've come to poison the spring
The soldiers decide to deal
Justly:
So they hang them on a tree by the well.

5

On Kelly's land at Aughrim, all is the same
As the old people remember, and pray it will be,
Where his father grazed sheep, like all before him.

Mullen the herd, propped by a fallen tree,
His mouth scabbed and his cheeks pitted by pox,
Blows on a reed pipe a fatal melody.

Ripe seeds are bending the tall meadowstalks.
He stops, when the sun sparks on a cuirass,
A goatskin drum across the sheepwalk tucks.

Buff-coated horsemen jump the walls, and press
The bleating flock, while Kelly pleads for pay:
'By the Holy Virgin, give us gold, not brass!'

Raw lancers goad their footsore ewes away
With rancid udders drained by thriving lambs:
'Do you grudge men food who fight for you?' they say.

Soon they reach camp, where flies hover in swarms
On entrails at the bivouacs, and they smoke
The meat on spits, lice crawling in their uniforms.

Farmer and herd follow with crook and stick,
Their grey slack tweed coats tied with twists of straw,
Reeking of wool and sour milk and turf smoke,

Up hill through hedgegaps to an ancient rath
Embanked by hawthorn, where the Catholic flag
Blazoned with Bourbon lilies for St Ruth

Floats white and gold above a deep red bog,
And here they halt, blessing themselves, and kneel:
'Christ make the Frenchman pay us for our flock!'

Inside, they see a hand with a swan quill
That writes and writes, while powdered clerks translate,
Quoting with foreign voice the general's will:

'Children, I bring from France no better aid
To toast the image-wreckers on hell fire
Than my own skill to lead your just crusade.

It is your duty, since I wage this war
For your soul's sake, to lose your flock, but win
A victory for your conscience and my honour.'

'Give back our fleeces!' begs the shepherd, then
St Ruth's head rises: '*Foutez-moi le camp!*'
Guards clash steel halberds, and the natives run.

Through glacial eskar, by the river Suck
They choose the bog path to the richer camp
With tongues to talk and secret prayers for luck.

All day packhorses laden westwards tramp
Trundling bronze cannon behind casques of shot,
While eastwards, armed with spite, two traitors limp.

The Danish mercenaries they chance to meet
Standing in hogweed, sheltered by a ditch,
Assume they're spies, with no one to translate,

So fetch them to a grey house, where the Dutch
Commander who serves England's Orange king
Shakes hands, and gives them each a purse to clutch,

While a blond adjutant runs off to bring
The gunner Finch, who'll need their eyes next day,
When the cold cannon mouths start uttering.

6

'They pick us for our looks
To line up with matchlocks,
Face shot like sand-bags,
Fall, and manure the grass
Where we wouldn't be let trespass
Alive, but to do their work
Till we dropped in muck.

Who cares which foreign king
Governs, we'll still fork dung,
No one lets *us* grab soil:
Roman or English school
Insists it is God
Who must lighten our burden
Digging someone else's garden.'

7

'I share a tent with Dan, smelling of seals
Whose oil he smears on his French matchlock
Drooling idly for hours about camp girls.

Polishing his plug bayonet, he boasts he'll hack
From a shorn heretic a pair of testicles
To hang above St Brigid's well for luck.

29

Soft west wind carries our friary bells
Against the tide of psalms flooding the plain.
Now Dan fills a powderhorn, his cheek swells.

"Learn him our creed," he says, "garotte your man:
Tomorrow night we'll eat like generals."
Our supper meat is prodded, sniffed by Dan.'

8

God was eaten in secret places among the rocks
His mother stood in a cleft with roses at her feet
And the priests were whipped or hunted like stags.

God was spoken to at table with wine and bread
The soul needed no heavenly guide to intercede
And heretics were burnt at stakes for what they said.

God was fallen into ruins on the shores of lakes
Peasants went on milking cows or delving dikes
And landlords corresponded with landlords across bogs.

'Seven candles in silver sticks,
Water on an oval table,
The painted warts of Cromwell
Framed in a sullen gold.
There was ice on the axe
When it hacked the king's head.
Moths drown in the dripping wax.

Slow sigh of the garden yews
Forty years planted.
May the God of battle
Give us this day our land
And the papists be trampled.
Softly my daughter plays
Sefauchi's Farewell.

Dark night with no moon to guard
Roads from the rapparees,
Food at a famine price,
Cattle raided, corn trod,
And the servants against us
With our own guns and swords.
Stress a hymn to peace.

Quiet music and claret cups,
Forty acres of green crops
Keep far from battle
My guest, with a thousand troops
Following his clan-call,
Red-mouthed O'Donnell.
I bought him: the traitor sleeps.

To whom will the land belong
This time tomorrow night?
I am loyal to fields I have sown
And the king reason elected:
Not to a wine-blotted birth-mark
Of prophecy, but hard work
Deepening the soil for seed.'

10

Out of the earth, out of the air, out of the water
And slinking nearer the fire, in groups they gather:
Once he looked like a bird, but now a beggar.

This fish rainbows out of a pool: 'Give me bread!'
He fins along the lake-shore with the starved.
Green eyes glow in the night from clumps of weed.

The water is still. A rock or the nose of an otter
Jars the surface. Whistle of rushes or bird?
It steers to the bank, it lands as a pikeman armed.

With flint and bundles of straw a limestone hall
Is gutted, a noble family charred in its sleep,
And they gloat by moonlight on a mound of rubble.

The highway trees are gibbets where seventeen rot
Who were caught last week in a cattle-raid.
The beasts are lowing. 'Listen!' 'Stifle the guard!'

In a pinewood thickness an earthed-over charcoal fire
Forges them guns. They melt lead stripped from a steeple
For ball. At the whirr of a snipe each can disappear

Terrified as a bird in a gorse-bush fire,
To delve like a mole or mingle like a nightjar
Into the earth, into the air, into the water.

III
DURING

I

St Ruth trots on a silver mare
Along the summit of the ridge,
Backed by a red cavalcade
Of the King's Life Guards.
He wears a blue silk tunic,
A white lace cravat,
Grey feathers in his hat.

He has made up his mind to put
The kingdom upon a fair combat:
Knowing he cannot justify
Losing Athlone
Before his Most Christian master,
He means to bury his body
In Ireland, or win.

The army commander only speaks
French and Italian:
In ranks below colonel
His army only speaks Irish.
When he gives an order
His jowls bleach and blush
Like a turkeycock's dewlap.

Lieutenant-General Charles Chalmont,
Marquis of St Ruth,
The Prince of Condé's disciple
In the music of war,
Jerks with spinal rapture
When a volley of musket-fire
Splits his ear.

Picture his peregrine eyes,
A wife-tormentor's thin
Heraldic mouth, a blue
Stiletto beard on his chin,
And a long forked nose
Acclimatized to the sulphurous
Agony of Huguenots.

He keeps his crab-claw tactics
Copied from classical books
An unbetrayable secret
From his army of Irishmen.
He rides downhill to correct
A numerical mistake
In his plan's translation.

He throws up his hat in the air,
The time is near sunset,
He knows victory is sure,
One cavalry charge will win it.
'*Le jour est à nous, mes enfants*,'
He shouts. The next minute
His head is shot off.

2

Mullen had seen St Ruth riding downhill
And Kelly held a taper. 'There's the Frenchman!'
Finch laid the cannon, a breeze curved the ball.

The victory charge was halted. Life-guards stooped down
And wrapped the dripping head in a blue cloak,
Then wheeled and galloped towards the setting sun.

Chance, skill and treachery all hit the mark
Just when the sun's rod tipped the altar hill:
The soldiers panicked, thinking God had struck.

3

Sarsfield rides a chestnut horse
At the head of his regiment,
His mountainous green shoulders
Tufted with gold braid,
Over his iron skull-piece
He wears the white cockade.
A bagpipe skirls.

Last summer after the Boyne
When King James had run,
He smashed the Dutch usurper's
Wagon-train of cannon
Benighted at Ballyneety.
Patrick Sarsfield, Earl of Lucan
Commands the reserve today.

The saviour of Limerick knows
Nothing of St Ruth's plan,
Not even that the battle
Of Aughrim has begun.
He has obeyed since dawn
The order to wait for further
Orders behind the hill.

He sees men run on the skyline
Throwing away muskets and pikes,
Then horsemen with sabres drawn
Cutting them down.
He hears cries, groans and shrieks.
Nothing he will do, or has done
Can stop this happening.

4

Comely their combat
            amidst death and wounds,
Romantic their disregard
            for cosmic detail:
The wrong kegs of ball
            were consigned to the castle,
Irish bullets too large
            for French firelocks.
A great stronghold
            became a weakness.

Till sunset they loaded
       muskets with tunic buttons
To fire on cavalry:
       squadron after squadron
Crossed the causeway
       and flanked their front.
Heroic volleys
       continued until nightfall:
They fell with no quarter
       when the battle was lost.

5

Luttrell on a black charger
At the rear of his regiment
Stands idle in a beanfield
Protected by a tower.
He wears a dandy yellow coat,
A white-feathered hat
And a gilded sabre.

When he hears the word spread
Along the line, 'St Ruth is dead,'
He retreats at a trot:
Leading his priding cavalry
To betray the humble foot:
Ten miles to a dinner, laid
In a mansion, then to bed.

6

Night covers the retreat.
Some English troops beating a ditch for loot
Capture a wounded boy. 'Don't shoot!'

'What'll we do with him?'
'I'll work in the camp.' 'Strip him!'
Naked he kneels to them. They light a lamp.

'Pretty boy.' 'Castrate the fucker!'
'Let the papist kiss my flute.'
'Toss a coin for the privilege to bugger . . .'

He cries like a girl. 'Finish him off.'
'No, keep him alive to be our slave.'
'Shove a sword up his hole.' They laugh.

A tipsy officer calls out:
'You men be on parade at eight.
I want no prisoners, d'you hear me? Shoot

The crowd we took ,when it gets light.
We've no more food. Goodnight.
God knows you all put up a splendid fight.'

IV
AFTER

A wolfhound sits under a wild ash
Licking the wound in a dead ensign's neck.

When guns cool at night with bugles in fog
She points over the young face.

All her life a boy's pet.
Prisoners are sabred and the dead are stripped.

Her ear pricks like a crimson leaf on snow,
The horse-carts creak away.

Vermin by moonlight pick
The tongues and sockets of six thousand skulls.

She pines for his horn to blow
To bay in triumph down the track of wolves.

Her forelegs stand like pillars through a siege,
His Toledo sword corrodes.

Nights she lopes to the scrub
And trails back at dawn to guard a skeleton.

Wind shears the berries from the rowan tree,
The wild geese have flown.

She lifts her head to cry
Like a woman keens in a famine for her son.

A redcoat, stalking, cocks
His flintlock when he hears the wolfhound growl.

Her fur bristles with fear at the new smell,
Snow has betrayed her lair.

'I'll sell you for a packhorse
You antiquated bigoted papistical bitch!'

She springs: in self-defence he fires his gun.
People remember this.

By turf embers she gives tongue
When the choirs are silenced in wood and stone.

2

(The Reverend George Story concludes
An Impartial History)

'I never could learn what became of St Ruth's corpse:
Some say he was left stript amongst the dead,
When our men pursued beyond the hill;
And others that he was thrown into a Bog:
However, though the man had an ill character
As a great persecutor of Protestants in France,
Yet we must allow him to be very brave in his person,
And indeed considerable in his conduct,
Since he brought the Irish to fight a better battle
Than ever that people could boast of before:
They behaved themselves like men of another nation.

But it was always the genius of this people
To rebel, and their vice was laziness.
Since first they began to play their mad pranks
There have died, I say, in this sad kingdom,
By the sword, famine and disease,
At least one hundred thousand young and old.
Last July alone, more execution was done
At Aughrim than in all Europe besides.
Seen from the top of the hill, the unburied dead
Covered four miles, like a great flock of sheep.

What did the mere Irish ever gain
By following their lords into rebellion?
Or what might they have gotten by success
But absolute servitude under France?
They are naturally a lazy crew
And love nothing more than to be left at ease.
Give one a cow and a potato garden
He will aspire to no greater wealth
But loiter on the highway to hear news.
Lacking plain honesty, but most religious,
Not one in twenty works, the gaols are full
Of thieves, and beggars howl on every street.
This war has ended happily for us:
The people now must learn to be industrious.'

3

Luttrell, Master of Luttrellstown
Sat in a gold and red sedan
The burden of a hungry urchin
And a weak old man
Barefoot on cobbles in the midnight rain,
Up torchlit quays from a coffee shop
Where after supper, the silver cup
Lifted, a fop had said
'It's time to bury Aughrim's dead.'

A poor smell of ordure
Seeped through his embroidered chair,
He slid the glass open for air,
Waved off a beggar groping at the door
And watched six black dray-horses cross
The river. 'Let the traitor pass.'
He felt his pocket full of pebbles
Which he used at Mass in straw-roofed chapels
To lob at little girls.

The chair slewed at his town house,
Flambeaus, footmen in place,
And plunked him down.
He'd sold his country to preserve his class,
The gutters hissed: but that was done
Twenty-six years ago, he said,
Had they not buried Aughrim's dead?
Standing under grey cut stone
A shadow cocked a gun.

No one betrayed his assassin
Although the Duke of Bolton
Offered three hundred pounds' reward.
The crowd spat on Henry Luttrell's coffin.
Eighty years after his murder
Masked men, inspired by Wolfe Tone,
Burst open his tomb's locks,
Lit a stub of wax
And smashed the skull with a pickaxe.

4

Sarsfield, great-uncle in the portrait's grime,
Your emigration built your fame at home.
Landlord who never racked, you gave your rent
To travel with your mounted regiment.

Hotly you duelled for our name abroad
In Restoration wig, with German sword,
Wanting a vicious murder thrust to prove
Your Celtic passion and our Lady's love.

Gallant at Sedgemoor, cutting down for James
The scythe-armed yokels Monmouth led like lambs,
You thought it needed God's anointed king
To breathe our Irish winter into spring.

Your ashwood lance covered the Boyne retreat:
When the divine perfidious monarch's rout
From kindred enemy and alien friend
Darkened the land, you kindled Ireland.

At Limerick besieged, you led the dance:
'If this had failed, I would have gone to France.'
When youths lit brandy in a pewter dish
You were their hazel nut and speckled fish.

A French Duke scoffed: 'They need no cannonballs
But roasted apples to assault these walls.'
Sarsfield, through plague and shelling you held out;
You saved the city, lost your own estate.

Shunning pitched battle was your strategy:
You chose rapparee mountain routes to try
The enemy's morale, and blew his train
Of cannon skywards in the soft night rain.

Your king, who gave St Ruth supreme command,
Mistrusted you, native of Ireland.
'Await further orders,' you were told
At Aughrim, when your plan was overruled.

You stood, while brother officers betrayed
By going, and six thousand Irish died.
Then you assumed command, but veered about:
Chose exile in your courteous conqueror's boat.

'Change kings with us, and we will fight again,'
You said, but sailed off with ten thousand men;
While women clutched the hawsers in your wake,
Drowning—it was too late when you looked back.

Only to come home stronger had you sailed:
Successes held you, and the French prevailed.
Coolly you triumphed where you wanted least,
On Flemish cornfield or at Versailles feast.

Berwick the bastard sired by James the Shit
Immortalized you with no head but grit.
He took your widow Honor for his wife
When serving the Sun King you lost your life.

We loved you, horseman of the white cockade,
Above all, for your last words, 'Would to God
This wound had been for Ireland.' Cavalier,
You feathered with the wild geese our despair.

5

Strangers visit the townland:
Called after wild geese, they fly through Shannon.

They know by instinct the sheepwalk
As it was before the great hunger and the exodus:

Also this cool creek of traitors.
They have come here to seek out ancestors.

They have read that the wind
Carried their forbears' gunsmoke, to make blind

The enemy, but nevertheless the Lord
Permitted the wicked to purify the good.

They know little about God
But something of the evil exploded by the word.

They are at the navel of an island
Driving slowly into well-drained battleground,

To follow the glacial eskar
By the new signpost to the credal slaughter,

Blood on a stone altar:
Seed, there should be seed, buried in a cairn.

If they listen, they may hear
Doubtless the litany of their houseled father.

Soon they locate the dun
Where St Ruth spun the thread of his fatal plan:

They try to imagine
Exactly what took place, what it could mean,

Whether by will or by chance:
Then turn in time to catch a plane for France.

THE GOD WHO
EATS CORN

WILLIAM LINDSAY MURPHY
1887-1965

NOTE

At the end of the nineteenth century there was no word in the language of the Matabele to describe the white man who came to settle in Central Africa, so he was called 'the god who eats corn', meaning that although he had godlike powers, he had to eat, and to die. My father, who was born in an Irish Rectory, retired from the British Colonial Service as Governor of the Bahamas, and settled in Southern Rhodesia in 1950 on virgin land, where he established a farm and later a school for African children. The time is the last year of Federation—and the myth of 'partnership'—1963.

I

In his loyal garden, like Horace's farm,
He asks his visitors to plant a tree.
The black shadow of the African msasa
Squats among the lawn's colonial company.

In honour among watersprays that spin
Rainbows over cool English rose-beds
Hand-weeded by a pink-soled piccanin
The Queen Mother's cypress nods in a straw hood.

The trees are labelled: a chairman of mines
Gave this copper beech, that silver oak
Was trowelled by a Governor: great names
Written on tags, Llewellin and Tredgold.

Livingstone's heir presented this wild fig
From the burnt-out forest of Africa:
On its branches by moonlight a boomslang swings.
This Cape creeper has a cold blue flower.

As a son I choose the native candelabra:
Perched on an ant-hill, after years of drought,
From its cut spines a milky sap flows:
To my father I give this tree as a tribute.

His own plane-tree, brought by seed from Cos,
From shade where Hippocrates swore his oath,
Wilts in the voodoo climate, while gums
The trekkers imported have sapped the earth.

Under these trees, he believes that indaba*
Could heal the blood-feud. Bull-frogs crackle
In the lily-pond. Tolerant water
Eases roots, and cools the racial fever.

II

From his green study half-door he looks out
On the young plantation of his old age:
An ibis is perched on a cone hut,
Rain-birds croak in the citrus orchard.

Boys are sharpening pangas at the wood-pile:
Trailers approach, filling barns from the field
With limp tobacco to be dried by steam.
A Union Jack droops on the school flag-pole.

Hunkered on dust in kaffir quarters
With rickety babies, the sewing-club meets
My mother bringing gifts through trellis doors
Frail as a lily in her straw sun-hat.

Such tinkle of bangles, such ivory teeth
Clacking, they gossip of clothes and clinics.
A child rolls a pram-wheel over the earth,
A cat is stalking the cooped-up chickens.

* *In tribal society, the chieftain decided his policy after hearing advice from his counsellors in the shade of a large tree. This counsel was called the indaba. The tree could be any kind of large African tree, a mopani, a fig, or, most likely, a msasa, a lovely deciduous tree of the bush.*

He drives to the store to collect his *Times*
And letters from home, tulip-trees in flower,
Road-grit on his tongue, tobacco booms
A memory, hot wind raising a dust-choked roar.

He swims before breakfast in a blue pool
Sometimes recalling Atlantic light
Splashed on to hymn-books in a pitch-pine hall
Where his father preached. He prays at night.

At the carol-service in the grading-shed
He reads the lesson, joining trade with truth.
My knees remember his coconut mats,
The mesh of our duty to improve the earth.

III

'To do some good for this poor Africa'
Was Livingstone's prayer, but not the Founder's dream.
Towards gold and diamonds, the Pioneer Column
Trekked at the bidding of a childless millionaire.

They came with ox-wagons, claiming a treaty,
To the king's kraal, his great indaba tree,
With charming letters from Queen Victoria:
There the chameleon swallowed the black fly.

In dusty dorps they slept with slave-girls,
On farms they divided the royal herd.
In stifling mine-shafts the disarmed warriors
Were flogged to work, their grazing-grounds wired.

So now at white homesteads, the coffee steams
On creepered verandahs. Racial partners
Do not mix in wedlock sons and daughters.
The white man rides: the black man is his horse.

Brown bare feet slide softly over the tiles
Soothing the master, scrubbing his bath,
Folding his towels, timidly with smiles
Smoothing his pillow, and wincing at his wrath.

To each black, his ten acres for millet;
To each white, his three thousand of grass.
The gospel of peace preached from the pulpit;
From the hungry fields the gospel of force.

IV

In a paradise for white gods he grows old
Cutting rafters out of the felled wood,
Baking bricks from the clay of ant-hills:
He plants the first rose on the burnt sandveld.

Thirteen years ago his books were unpacked
In the path of mambas, where nomads' fires
Lit stone-age sketches on the walls of caves
And the sand was printed by lion spoor.

His Governor's helmet stowed in a teak chest,
He called back Homer after forty years'
Damp decay in the West of Ireland:
He retired into sunlight on a thousand acres.

Trapped from tribes in their idle forest
Negroes gathered to work for meal and poll-tax,
Their teeming women overcrawled by bony kids,
Calling him 'Baas', grinning, hungry, diseased.

They wove wicker-and-mud hovels to sleep in.
Tractors invaded the elephant road.
A bore-hole was sunk. Cicadas at his fly-screen
Halted and shrilled. The kudu retreated.

He fed corn to his gang and cured fever.
Cigarettes sold in a London shop
Kept people stooped on his kopje alive.
Each year he felled more trees to plant a crop.

Between the auction floors and seed-bed sowing
First in a thatched hut he began a school.
The market rose and fell, drought followed flooding,
When the leaves ripened there were showers of hail.

Daily at dawn, they clang the plough-disc gong
That winds a chain of men through vleis and veld.
No boss-boy drives them with a sjambok's thong.
At dusk they come to class-rooms to be schooled.

Children are chanting hymns, their lean bodies
Tropically sensual behind puritan desks,
From mealie plot and swamp of tsetse flies
Lured by the witchcraft of the god's mechanics.

A red-hot poker flowers in the playground,
A viper sleeps on the sand. The dry slate
Under the sweating palm is rubbed and scrawled.
They wait like logs, ready for fire and wind.

V

Tall in his garden, shaded and brick-walled,
He upholds the manners of a lost empire.
Time has confused dead honour with dead guilt
But lets a sunbird sip at a gold creeper.

His scholar's head, disguised in a bush hat,
Spectacled eyes, that watch the weaver's nest
Woven, have helped a high dam to be built
Where once the Zambesi was worshipped and wasted.

Sometimes he dreams of a rogue elephant
That smashed the discharged rifle in his hand:
Or reading, remembers the horns of buffalo,
The leopards he shipped to the Dublin zoo.

On the game-cleared plateau the settlers say
'This is our home: this is white man's country'.
Dust-storms gather to hide their traces
Under boulders balanced in a smouldering sky.

VI

They say, when the god goes, the rain falls,
Contour ridges burst, sweeping off crops,
The rafters crumble, trees shoot through floors,
And wind carves the fields into smooth dust-heaps.

The concrete cracks and the brown rivers bleed,
Cattle die of rinderpest, dogs with rabies
Bite their masters, the half-freed slaves are freed
But not into a garden that anyone remembers.

Now the old mopani forest is felled.
The settlers try to cling to their laagers,
Wire for a gun-boat, profit in gold-shares,
Dream of silk flags and showers of assegais.

The trees that fail are soon devoured by ants.
Sundowners bind together a white crowd:
Some preach of partners, more sneer at the Munts
Getting cheeky, lazier than ever. He's bored.

While he prepares to fly to Ithaca
The B.S.A. police hold rifle drill,
Pyres kindle under *Pax Britannica*.
He stays to build a club-room for the school.

At dusk on the stoep he greets ambassadors
From Kenya and Ceylon. The silver trays
Are lit by candles cupped in the flower borders.
Husks hang on his dry indaba trees.

Last thing at night he checks the rain-gauge
Remembering his father on a rectory lawn.
Thunder is pent in the drums of the compound.
He feels too old to love the rising moon.